Cottagecore

SIMPLIFIED

COTTAGECORE SIMPLIFIED

13-Digit ISBN: 978-1-64643-431-2
10-Digit ISBN: 1-64643-431-5

This book may be ordered by mail from the publisher.
Please include $5.99 for postage and handling.
Please support your local bookseller first!

Books published by Cider Mill Press Book Publishers are
available at special discounts for bulk purchases in the United
States by corporations, institutions, and other organizations.
For more information, please contact the publisher.

Cider Mill Press Book Publishers
"Where good books are ready for press"
501 Nelson Place
Nashville, Tennessee 37214

cidermillpress.com

Typography: Bookeyed Jack, Sofia Pro, Sweet Sans Pro

Vectors used under official license from Shutterstock.com.
Images used under official license from Shutterstock.com,
Unsplash.com, and Pexels.com.

Printed in India

23 24 25 26 27 REP 5 4 3 2 1
First Edition

Cottagecore

SIMPLIFIED

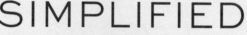

A GUIDE TO COUNTRYSIDE CHARM, COMFORT & HAPPINESS

BY KATIE MERRIMAN

CIDER MILL PRESS

BOOK PUBLISHERS

Contents

1

What Is Cottagecore?

*C*lose your eyes. Imagine you are standing outside, looking up toward a small brick cottage.
Ivy is crawling up the sides toward the shingled
roof. It's surrounded by lush green grass and a beautiful garden, almost overflowing with wildflowers.
Walking around to the back of the cottage, you
hear the sounds of various animals: soft clucking
from chickens, tramps from hooves on grass as cows
graze, and little splashes from a pond occupied by
a couple of geese peacefully swimming. The windows to the house are open, and rosemary bread sits
on a windowsill, smelling like a dream, fresh from
an old stone oven. When you open the front door,
you're surrounded with warmth and that wonderful
cozy feeling. To your right you see the living room,
well loved and enjoyed, with art projects and crafts
laid out on a wooden coffee table that must be an
antique. You finger through the items on the table:
a half-knitted garment, some well-used paints, and
a well-worn copy of *Anne of Green Gables*. On the

walls there's a gallery of art prints, and despite the obvious mixing and matching, they complement one another beautifully. To your left is the entryway to the kitchen. On the counter you see baking supplies all askew—the leftovers from the rosemary bread. Near the windowsill is a small herb garden; you spot rosemary, basil, and thyme growing happily within. Turning around, you walk straight past the kitchen and living room toward the bedroom. It's a soft space, with candles and books everywhere. Looking through the closet, you notice that all of the garments are unique. It's unclear which time period they belonged to. You pull out dresses with puffed sleeves, midlength skirts, and neutral colors. Perhaps a few have floral or nature-inspired motifs. Rubbing the material between your fingers, you notice that each piece is made of cotton or linen fabric. Reflecting on the whole space, you are reminded of an idealized version of a countryside grandmother's house: cozy and warm, eclectic, and finished with homemade touches. This is Cottagecore, the idea of country living in the most romantic of senses.

With that, I wish you a very warm welcome to *Cottagecore Simplified*, which is truly a very fitting title for a movement that is all about simplicity, slow living, and romanticization. Throughout this little book, you'll dive into the idyllic world of

Cottagecore. I'll overview the Cottagecore movement, its aesthetic appeal, how to achieve it, and how to engage with the lifestyle, and we'll conclude with a little bit about Cottagecore in practice, both online and in real life.

Cottagecore is an aesthetic and lifestyle movement that was popularized throughout 2020 and 2021, although its origins date back to 2018. The aesthetic idealizes a simpler, rural lifestyle that encourages slowness, romanticism, and simplicity. Departing from the hustle and bustle and the go-go-go, and instead embracing each moment and enjoying the little things in life—this is the core ideology of Cottagecore. Cottagecore has exploded in popularity, particularly among young people, although this lifestyle is not only for the young; people from all walks of life are engaging in Cottagecore. Looking through Cottagecore content on social media, you will see plenty of creators in their midtwenties or early thirties, but you'll also see many people of all ages. Cottagecore tends to attract people who are tired of all work and no play, those who appreciate nature, and those who are keen to learn new things and explore. However, there are different levels of exploration. You certainly don't need to move into a cottage in order to be Cottagecore. Many readers may be practicing Cottagecore and not even know it! Perhaps

enjoying your morning coffee while listening to an audiobook is your favorite part of the day, or you have an affinity for old-fashioned clothing—these are all possible aspects of a Cottagecore life.

With over 4.2 million posts associated with #Cottagecore on Instagram and 12 billion views on TikTok, it's fair to say the aesthetic has made quite a splash. Cottagecore was primed to be successful for several reasons, the first being that people are tired; more and more conversations are being held around mental health and burnout, and people are looking for an escape. This only intensified during the COVID-19 lockdowns. For many, being cooped up was extremely challenging. For some of those people, this sparked hopes and dreams of having space and opportunity to expand, to be able to slow down and take a breather in nature, to forget all of their worries. On top of all of this, people are more conscious than ever about sustainability and being eco-friendly, which absolutely aligns with Cottagecore's key tenants of harmonizing with nature and slow living. All of these factors combined made it the perfect movement for this moment.

As a lifestyle, Cottagecore may seem like a strange new phenomenon, but the idea of escaping to an idyllic country-style life is not new; in fact, even Marie Antoinette had Cottagecore fantasies. She had her own rustic retreat built on the grounds of Versailles called Hameau de la Reine, or the Queen's Hamlet. While in residence at the Queen's Hamlet, Marie Antoinette would host her friends for an intimate social experience. They would wear sun hats and dress more casually than they would at court. Most of us are not escaping from the grandeur of Versailles, but it's clear that embracing the simple and slow lifestyle is an innate desire for many people. There are even modern-day celebrities who have chosen a slower, rural-inspired lifestyle, like Julia Roberts and Amanda Seyfried, who both own farms with animals and barnyards to take care of.

I'm Katie, a Canadian librarian who has identified with Cottagecore since early 2020, although I was certainly interested in many of the aspects of Cottagecore well before it was named. I've been a Cottagecore content creator since 2020, sharing my journey with a community of people who are interested in my Cottagecore lifestyle, fashion, and personality. How did I get started? Well, I've always been a reader with a particular interest in historical stories, forever wishing I could be Elizabeth Bennet just for a day! Self-expression has always been important to me, which I convey through my fashion; I learned how to sew as a teenager. I have a fond memory of sewing myself a floral midi skirt when I was 19. I wanted one desperately, but I couldn't find a single store that sold them. The first time I wore it out, I remember walking around my university's campus and feeling like people were very perplexed by my choice. At the time, only mini or maxi skirts were popular, and for whatever reason, the mid length was seen as the oddest of options. But I was over the moon with the skirt, feeling like a character from a fairy tale.

Since I was young, I always invested in my imagination. As teenagers, my sister and I would have themed photo shoots where we would dress up in costumes or elaborate ensembles. We'd wear the pieces I never had the courage to wear in any other context. It wasn't until the end of my undergraduate schooling that I really started developing a unique style that would eventually lead me to Cottagecore.

I started my master's degree in librarian sciences in 2017, and my favorite librarian was always Evelyn O'Connell, from the 1999 film *The Mummy*. Her historical 1920s academic outfits inspired me, and I knew I wanted to look just like her. So I began dressing to suit this historic librarian aesthetic. Within this period, dressing "vintage" had become a very popular niche internet fashion choice. It was in these years between 2017 and 2019 that I began dressing "vintage inspired," which I believe was a direct precursor to Cottagecore for many people. Since Cottagecore has historical roots, going from vintage inspired (which is basically dressing in any modern clothing that looks like it's from a certain historical era) to Cottagecore is a very easy and natural transition, clothingwise.

It was during this time that my life became hectic. Not only was I a full-time grad student, but I was also working three jobs. This go-go-go lifestyle very quickly became overwhelming, and my body began begging for a break. I had stopped making time for the things that made me happy, like reading, crafting, and nature. I had only just finished school and was working for several months before the COVID lockdowns, and my life was forced to pause. All of this primed me to be curious about Cottagecore; a historically inspired style that advocated for slow living seemed to be the exact niche I needed to explore. Several of the vintage creators I had already been following also began using the hashtags around Cottagecore. I had never felt so strongly connected to the style or message. I eventually decided that I'd try sharing my outfits publicly, as well as little pieces of my life. I started sewing again and shared that with my followers too! Now I'm not only an observer in the community, but contributing to it.

How can you become Cottagecore? Well, read on to find out!

How Cottagecore are you?

Check off the boxes that apply to you!

☐ You take time to enjoy the little things.

☐ You've always had an affinity for aprons, bandanas, and baskets.

☐ You've been told you remind someone of their grandmother.

☐ You love being in nature.

☐ You want to learn to knit, crochet, or sew.

☐ A slow evening in sounds like an ideal night.

☐ A cottage in the woods is your dream home.

☐ You have a firm belief that you cannot have too many florals.

☐ A picnic with friends is an ideal day.

☐ You love frogs and mushrooms.

1–3: Cottagecore beginner
You're interested in Cottagecore, and you already have some Cottagecore tendencies. You likely have to take time to slow down and enjoy each moment. Try not to worry about the constant stressors and to-do lists—instead, focus on enjoying and romanticizing your life. Maybe try out a new hobby, like embroidery!

4–6: Cottagecore intrigued
You've likely got the aesthetics and some of the interests in the bag, but you may be scared to take some of those fashion risks or wear things that may be considered unusual. Don't be afraid to follow your heart and do the things that may scare you! Or perhaps you've only partaken in the aesthetic dress. In that case, maybe you can try engaging in some Cottagecore hobbies!

7–8: Cottagecore aficionado
You've got the style, you've got the lifestyle, you follow the hashtags, and your TikTok For You page has about a dozen women running through fields and knitting in cozy cottages. Maybe it's time to start your own Cottagecore social media page!

9–10: Cottagecore expert
Okay, you could have written this book. You only bought it to validate how Cottagecore you already are—admit it!

2

Cottagecore Aesthetics

Historical Roots

Where does Cottagecore come from? What are the inspirations? The heart of Cottagecore comes from the fantasy of escaping to the countryside, a rural life often associated with a "simpler" historical time. Imagine something like the Disney princesses before they found their princes and ball gowns. Many who dress in Cottagecore style use these concepts for inspiration, although there are definitely modern interpretations of Cottagecore dress too.

Clothing and Style

There are so many interesting and exciting aspects of Cottagecore, but it would be impossible to deny that the aesthetic appeal is a mainstay for many people, inspiring millions of posts across social media. Cottagecore may seem like a complicated aesthetic, requiring unobtainable pieces or extraordinarily expensive garments. None of that has to be true! Let's simplify the fashion aspect of Cottagecore.

Before going out and buying a dozen new Cottagecore outfits, you should understand that one of the most fundamental aspects of Cottagecore fashion is the concept of slow fashion. Slow fashion is the opposite of fast fashion. Fast fashion is the most common method of clothing production today. When you shop fast fashion, you're focusing on overconsumption, buying hauls of cheap clothing to follow every trend, and then throwing away those garments as quickly as you bought them once they're no longer in style. In the last decade, the number of garments produced and purchased has doubled, while the number of times a garment is worn has continued to decrease. Meanwhile, shopping slow fashion is about making the most out of each garment and making the most ethical purchases or clothing acquisitions possible. This doesn't mean you can't ever buy anything new; it means considering the pieces you already own and not focusing on bringing in new pieces with every new trend or interest. You'd be surprised how versatile pieces in your closet can be with a little bit of revision. There are likely many Cottagecore looks you can achieve without purchasing anything new!

If you need a little inspiration or you're feeling a bit tired of the pieces you have, check in with friends or family who might be looking to part with any garments, or suggest a closet swap. Check out your local thrift stores or their online equivalents, like Poshmark, Etsy, or Depop, to see what articles you can acquire without purchasing something never worn before. Being kind to the planet by making the most of what you have, thus avoiding overspending and overconsumption, is a fundamental aspect of Cottagecore. Of course, this doesn't mean you can't buy new garments. Simply consider this your first option, then determine what additional pieces are needed to complete the Cottagecore wardrobe of your dreams. When choosing to invest in new pieces, select well-made, classic, high-quality items that will likely stand the test of time and be more unique and special! For example, to treat myself I'll buy a made-to-measure linen dress on Etsy. It's much more affordable than you might think! Also remember that it's normal to take time to build your wardrobe. It took me well over a year to become fully happy with my Cottagecore wardrobe.

While there certainly are specific Cottagecore styles, that doesn't mean that you have to dress a certain way in order to be Cottagecore. You can live a Cottagecore lifestyle regardless of how you dress.

Clothes are only an enhancement; someone could dress in jeans and a T-shirt daily and still identify with a Cottagecore lifestyle—especially if the shirt has a frog on it. With that being said, there certainly is a clothing style commonly associated with Cottagecore, and many who embrace the aesthetic will follow these principles.

Elements to Look For

How does one put together a Cottagecore outfit? There are a few important things to consider. First and foremost:

Articles of clothing: Seek out overalls, dresses, midlength flowy skirts, peasant-style tops, pinafores, and oversized cardigans.

Fabrics: Look for natural fibers, cotton, linen, hemp, wool, and other similar materials. Not only do they visually match the Cottagecore aesthetic, but wearing natural fibers is also better for the environment, which is always a Cottagecore win. Natural fibers also tend to last longer than polyester garments and are generally wearable year-round.

Colors and patterns: Cottagecore isn't known for its extensive and bold display of colors. Look for soft, muted colors and earth tones—nothing bold or ostentatious. When it comes to patterns, look for delicate motifs like florals and patterns that are derived from nature. Plaids and ginghams are great as well!

Details: Pieces with embroidery, lace, and frills are perfect for Cottagecore styles. Garments with whimsical details like puffed sleeves or Puritan or Peter Pan collars are also great additions to a Cottagecore wardrobe. Look for elements that provide that little extra burst of femininity, historical flair, or celebration of nature.

Imagery: Much of the iconography in Cottagecore is related to or depicting barnyard or woodland animals (frogs in particular), mushrooms, candles, tea or teacups, and fruits or vegetables.

Accessories: Adding bandanas, wicker or straw purses, ribbons, or straw hats to any outfit is an easy way to create a Cottagecore look.

Shoes: We can't forget about shoes (that is, if you're not lazing about, dipping your toes in a stream)! Simple flats, classic or chunky Mary Janes, Victorian-style ankle boots, Oxfords, or Wellingtons are all shoes that fit the aesthetic.

Tips to Make Your Clothing Last Longer

Sweat guard undershirts

Nothing ruins a blouse faster than sweat stains. Protect your shirts by investing in sweatproof undershirts. This will provide an extra layer between you and the garment, so that it is protected from sweat and can be washed less frequently, preserving the piece!

Wash your clothes less

The more often you wash your clothes, the faster the piece will age. Here are some tips for washing that can help preserve your garments:

Use cool water to wash your clothes. This will help reduce wrinkles and prevent shrinkage and damage.

Hand wash. Any delicate pieces you own should be washed by hand, especially linen or cotton pieces. For linen pieces, you can even consider spot washing places that soil quickly, like the underarms, preserving the rest of the fabric.

Use a delicates bag. Any garments that have something that could snag or be snagged can be washed in delicate-garments bags to help preserve your pieces.

Mend garments

It can be so tempting to throw away a top after losing a button, or to tuck it away somewhere, saying you'll take it in to get fixed, until it's been two years and you realize you've stopped wearing it, so you just throw it away. We've all been there—that's why learning to sew buttons back on, repair small holes, or apply patches can add unique aesthetic elements to different garments and extend their life!

Fold heavy sweaters/knits

Did you know that hanging heavy knits can distort the shape of your sweaters? The weight of the sweater, especially if it's hung on a thin hanger, will pull the garment until its shape has shifted, damaging the integrity of the garment. It's considered best to fold heavy sweaters and other knits to help preserve their shape.

Steaming vs. ironing

Ironing can be very hard on garments. Whenever possible, use a steamer to dewrinkle garments rather than an iron.

Hair

With the outfits settled, we can move on to hairstyling.

HEATLESS CURLS

Heatless curls are an amazing way to get the perfect Cottagecore hair with minimal effort, time, and hair damage. Here are several methods and tips and tricks I've learned over the years.

DIY SOCK CURLS

If you're looking to try heatless curls tonight and haven't purchased anything, you're in luck! This method just requires two socks and a few bobby pins!

Take two clean ankle socks that you don't use anymore and cut off the toes. This should leave you with two short tubes with holes on either end. Roll them each up so that it looks almost like a scrunchie. Brush your hair, parting it down the middle with half on each side of your head. Take one side and pull the hair through one of the sock scrunchies placed on the top of your head. Wrap your hair around the sock scrunchie—your hair should be masking the scrunchie. Once you've wrapped it all up, use bobby pins and pin your hair against the scrunchie to keep everything in place. Do the same thing to the other side. The final result should look like two space buns on the top of your head.

Tip: The direction you wrap your hair will affect the direction of the curls. Do this just as you're about to go to bed, allowing the curls to sit for at least 6–8 hours. Gently undo them in the morning for loose curls that will fall to beachy waves throughout the day. The beauty of this style is the volume it gives, with your hair being placed on the top of your head. This is also a very sustainable and eco-friendly curling method! If your hair is shorter, try placing the socks at the back of your head behind your ears—this will allow you to put more hair into the curl pattern.

LEGGINGS/BATHROBE CURLS

This version of heatless curls will provide tighter curls.

Take a pair of leggings or your bathrobe tie. Take your hair in 1- to 1.5-inch sections and wrap it around the leggings or bathrobe tie, adding sections as you go. If you are using leggings, you should be wrapping the hair around the legs of the pants so that the butt portion sits on your head. Try to keep it relatively tight and close to the back of your head; you don't want the back sections to be too loose and end up not curling. Once you've finished wrapping, fasten the hair with either bobby pins, a scrunchie, or a hair tie. If you used a bathrobe tie, tie the ends around the back of your head to keep the rest of the tie out of your face. If you used leggings, you can fold the lower leg portion of the leggings over the wrapped hair to help protect and preserve the curl.

Tip: The thicker the item you use, the looser your curls will be. Leggings, likely being thicker than a bathrobe tie, will give looser curls. The more hair you have, the bigger the item may need to be. Use trial and error to see what works best for your hair type, thickness, and texture. Those with short hair may need to use more bobby pins to keep their ends from unraveling along the way down.

HALF-UP HALF-DOWN

To achieve this popular style, take the front sections of your hair and tie them at the back of your head. You can choose to leave face-framing pieces in the front if you'd like. There are a few things Cottagecore enthusiasts will use to jazz up this style, such as:

RIBBONS

Tie a ribbon or a large bow on the back piece. This creates a very soft and romantic look.

TWISTS

Twist the two front sections into a rope and tie them back in the twists. Feel free to pull at them slightly to give a bit of a messier look.

PINS

Instead of tying the hair back, consider pinning the front sections to the back sides of your head with a slight twist. This can create more volume in your hair while achieving the same look. You can also find stylized pins that can add a little extra flair; look for those with a nature motif on them.

BRAIDED STYLES

Good old classic braids! Whether it be a basic braid, pigtail braids, or French braids, braids are certainly Cottagecore and will add that timeless charm to your outfit.

MILKMAID BRAIDS

Milkmaid braids are two regular pigtail braids wrapped around the top of your head, instead of hanging down. To achieve this style when braiding, be conscious of braiding your hair in the direction you want them to go. Use copious amounts of bobby pins to keep the braids against your head, then fluff out the braids slightly by tugging on the outer parts of the braids to create a slightly messier look. Add flowers or leaves to your braids to heighten the Cottagecore vibes.

LOOPED TWIN BRAIDS

Braid your hair into two pigtails, braiding through to as close to the ends as possible. Pin one end up next to where the braid starts, creating a little loop. Repeat on the other side. To add a little flair, tie a ribbon around the base of the braid; this will also help the braided loop hold its place.

NATURAL HAIR

If you prefer to wear your hair natural, or if you have a longer-lasting style like braids, you can add that Cottagecore essence to your hair by adding flowers into your hair or using other dainty accessories like barrettes—look for those with pearls or nature motifs.

Overall tips:

- Don't expect to find the perfect heatless curls technique on your first try. It really can be a trial-and-error ordeal, but trust the process and you'll figure out the ideal setup in due course. Try taking notes on what works best for you, so your ideal method can be identified.

- Despite what I commonly see done, I've always had the most luck with heatless curls fresh after washing my hair, letting it dry ninety percent of the way (either by air-drying or blow-drying), and then tying it up for the night. If you try when your hair is wet or damp when putting it into the styles, most often your hair won't dry all the way through, leading to limp waves.

- Heatless curls will work best for people with natural waves to naturally curly hair. If your natural hair has difficulty holding a curl, these methods may be more difficult for you to achieve or master.

- Having long hair is required; most methods will work best if your hair is at least shoulder length. If you have short hair, you may need to modify these methods (or at least use more bobby pins!).

Cottagecore Looks

Now that we've considered some details of the Cottagecore aesthetic, let's take a moment to describe several different styles or looks.

Cottagecore Modern

For those new to Cottagecore or who may be nervous about fully committing to the aesthetic, an easy-to-wear Cottagecore look features overalls. First, you'll need to find a pair of light-wash overalls—even better if they're vintage! Pair the overalls with a puff-sleeve floral top. Slip on coordinating flats and pick some flowers to tuck into the pocket of your overalls for the finishing touches. If you'd like, tie your hair into two braids (*Anne of Green Gables* style), and you've got a beautiful Cottagecore look! These pieces are likely already sitting in most closets or are easily found at any thrift store. If this is too much for you, consider focusing on one great Cottagecore piece, and slowly work your way up to a more complete look as you feel more comfortable.

Cottagecore Cozy

Once you've become more engaged in Cottagecore, styles with dresses and skirts are a great next step. Pair a soft-patterned, flowy midi skirt with a simple fitted T-shirt or camisole, and layer an oversized cardigan on top to complete the outfit. For a little extra Cottagecore flair, tie a bandana in your hair and accessorize with a wicker purse. These accessories allude to the historical elements of the aesthetic. As for footwear, try some ankle boots with a frilly sock peeking out—altogether a quintessential Cottagecore look! For our Cottagecore men, you may want to try some linen pants with a button-up shirt, with Oxfords and a natural, gel-free hairstyle.

Cottagecore Royalty

What would a devotee of Cottagecore's outfits look like? These outfits may be harder to find at a thrift store or in friends' or family's closets. They most likely need to be purchased from a specialty designer who creates Cottagecore attire. Layer a midi-length pinafore-style dress over a statement-sleeved blouse, and ensure the blouse's collar is visible over the dress. Depending on the weather, you could wear a wide-brimmed straw hat with a chin tie, either on your head or around your neck (allowing the hat to lie against your back). As for shoes, a flat- or Victorian-style ankle boot would suit perfectly. A more masculine look might include a laced blouse and pantaloons with boots—the sort of outfit you might picture being worn by a pirate or a prince. These kinds of Cottagecore styles are where hardcore Cottagecore devotees shine, though they could be considered costume-y by your friends and family, who may not share your passion for the aesthetic.

Home Decor

Every Cottagecore lover's dream home is that little cottage in the woods. A small brick house with ivy crawling up the sides. Beautiful wildflowers and fat bumblebees buzzing from bloom to bloom. Inside, you're greeted by a sense of coziness, almost like a grandmother's house, but perfectly curated. The bookshelves are stacked with books and little knick-knacks, and plants are placed throughout the area. Of course, not every Cottagecore space is going to look like this, but in general this description inspires most decor choices. You can make any space into a Cottagecore haven, whether you live in a tiny studio apartment, want to make your bedroom your

Cottagecore sanctuary, or are fortunate enough to actually live in a cottage in the woods. Here are some tips to transform your space.

When bringing in pieces, look for elements such as:

- Wood finishes
- Brass
- Stone
- Brick
- Floral patterns
- Earth tones
- Muted colors
- Vintage items
- Books
- Clocks
- Cookware
- Art prints

Similarly to fashion, thrifting as much as you can is truly ideal when it comes to Cottagecore. It really is the most effective method for finding just the right piece. DIY is also a big component of Cottagecore. Found the perfect bookshelf at the thrift store, just not the right color? Paint it! There are so many ways to make something your own. Create your own art and decor pieces! Incorporating handmade art into your home adds that unique touch that's irreproducible—something special that makes the space truly yours. Try embroidering, or create a painting and display it on your wall; one thing Cottagecore is not is minimalist.

DIY Projects for Your Home

FRAMED PRESSED FLOWERS

Find some flowers that complement the decor and color of your space. Press them in clear frames and place them around your area. These little bursts of color will liven up your space and are a very easy way to create aesthetic pieces for your home.

MACRAMÉ PLANT HOLDERS

Plants are very Cottagecore, but we can up the Cottagecore factor even more by creating macramé plant holders. These holders are beautiful handmade pieces that are not only decorative but also useful!

EMBROIDERY

If embroidery is a hobby you're interested in, you might consider creating a gallery wall of embroidered pieces. Think of a cohesive theme and slowly work on each image until you've made a few you're proud of. Then hang them on your wall! You could even think of it as a little art gallery to display your recent work, and switch the pieces up every so often to show how you've improved! What a great homey and creative touch for your space.

DRIED WREATH

Create a dried wreath to hang on your wall. It's incredible what you can create with just a hot glue gun, hot glue stick, and some things from the great outdoors! Think of the season you want to represent, or just use flora local to your area to design something truly beautiful! Just be mindful if you have pets or small children that nothing is toxic.

DRIED ORANGE GARLAND

Perfect for the holidays or any time of year, a dried orange garland is a beautiful way to add a little muted color into your home. Simply thinly slice up some oranges and put them in the oven at about 225°F for a few hours, then string them all together. This project can be done in an afternoon, with things you likely already have in your home.

Cottagecore Home Vibes

Even within Cottagecore, there are different styles that speak to different people. A few of the most popular styles are:

Cozy

A cozy Cottagecore aesthetic would focus on the aspects that create an environment of warmth and ease. To achieve this kind of vibe, you want to bring lots of texture into your space. Find unique quilts, blankets, or rugs with texture or vintage-inspired patterns on them. Find warm wood elements to bring into the space; these can be the furniture or the art on the walls. Use warm lighting. Really focus on earth tones, leaning toward warmer hues. Look for plush furniture pieces with structural bits you can still sink into—think wide armchairs. When considering what art to put up, focus on things that you may have a personal connection to—images or items that represent a good memory or have a special place in your heart. These will help curate a warm and cozy Cottagecore vibe.

The most important room in a cozy Cottagecore home is the bedroom, innately the coziest space in a home. A big wooden bed frame is a classic. Look for a comforter that has a floral or gingham pattern. Be generous with the matching throw pillows. Don't be afraid to mix soft patterns—just ensure they have the same or complementary color palettes. Hang dried flowers or fairy lights around your bed or headboard. Bring in as many aesthetic candles as you can.

Historical

An ideal historically inspired Cottagecore space would be just like one you'd see in a Regency period drama. Think about those pieces that aren't just vintage but feel antique. Think: a wooden dresser with an immaculately carved pattern, or a Persian-inspired rug. A historical aesthetic may rely on DIY projects and sprucing up furniture or decor pieces you found thrifting.

The room you'll want to focus on in this style is the living room. You'll want to ensure that your space is filled with transformational pieces. Adding vintage items to your existing space is a great first step. Find worn books with nice covers, tall candles, and vintage furniture. Look for a Victorian-inspired couch; you'll be shocked by how much it transforms your surroundings, and how cheap a secondhand one can be! Tie in luxurious-looking pieces like gold mirrors with more homey-looking pieces, like candles and stacks of worn books. This contrast will help curate historical-inspired vibes, so it doesn't look like you're just re-creating a period drama. Making use of patterned wallpaper or muted colors will really elevate the space's uniqueness, or, if you're a little scared of that commitment, you can start with an accent wall. Maybe consider adding paneling too! Hang up a gallery wall of prints with contrasting frames. Play around with different finishes and frame shapes and sizes. Look for inspiration from your favorite period dramas and any historical houses nearby.

Farmstead

A Cottagecore farmstead may align closest with the majority's conception of what a Cottagecore home should look like. It's probably what we'd imagine our little cottage in the wood's interior to be like.

For this style, the most important room is the kitchen. Don't be afraid of color. The coziest farm-inspired kitchens have colored cabinets; think warm green and other inviting hues. A creamy white or natural wood works beautifully too. Bring in complementary-colored dish towels; the more you use them, the most aesthetic they become. Look for vintage dishware and cookware. Dish sets with farm animals or floral prints are perfect, and brass cookware hung for display adds to the visual effect. Make the space inviting by putting out fruits and veggies—bonus points if you grew them yourself, or at least went to the farmers market. Spend time finding a unique tea set. There are fun novelty tea sets that will complement the space beautifully. In a modern kitchen, there often isn't a focus on art, so switch it up and incorporate pieces featuring nature and its elements.

In all aspects of Cottagecore, being mindful of what we have and how to make the most of our pieces is very important. Before investing in multiple new items, consider how you can transform what you have already, or what you can add to the space to provide these Cottagecore touches. If you're ready to part with pieces, see if you can sell or give away your furniture, art, or other knickknacks. Try to look for secondhand pieces. I recommend looking at local thrift stores, flea markets, etc. Also try online places, like Facebook Marketplace, or secondhand e-commerce, like Poshmark. Use search terms like Cottagecore, antique, cozy, Victorian, and vintage to find pieces that may suit your style. Best of luck!

Community

If we could see into a Cottagecore devotee's heart, what would it look like?

Open and spacious: A Cottagecore heart is open to new experiences, meeting new people, and letting those things take space in its world and the wider world we share.

Soft and warm: In our modern world, strength is prized—strength of mind, strength of body—but those definitions of strong are generally quite strict. A Cottagecore heart is comfortable with softness. Being soft is its own type of strength. Being soft requires strength that acknowledges that you may be hurt, you may be vulnerable, but you're dedicated to being a comforting light for the world.

Colorful: While the Cottagecore community aesthetically prefers muted tones and earth tones, a Cottagecore heart is colorful like a child's. It is bright and full of life and vivacious energy.

Large and full of generosity: Someone with a Cottagecore heart wants to share joy, knowledge, and the things they create. Sharing what you've learned with friends, family, and even acquaintances aligns with the core values of Cottagecore.

If someone is beginning their baking journey, you can offer advice on how they could improve, while providing encouragement for their current efforts. If you meet a new knitter, ask them if they'd like to be a part of your knitting circle. Share your efforts and energies with people, and you'll receive theirs in return.

The Cottagecore community is something special, that's for sure. A community based in slowness and calmness, and one that appreciates the little moments. It's a community that's open to everyone. If you explore Cottagecore hashtags on social media, you'll soon find people who identify as Cottagecore across North America, Europe, Asia, and the whole world. Even though aspects of the style are based on imaginings of a European historical landscape, you'll find people in Japan wearing midi dresses with embroidered collars, enjoying nature, using Cottagecore hashtags and identifying with the Cottagecore community. Or someone from Brazil might share their homemade bread recipe to express their love of baking. This to say there's no one way to be Cottagecore; anyone in any stage of life and of any race, ethnicity, or gender identity can look and be Cottagecore.

What's your Cottagecore aesthetic?

What's your go-to outfit?
  A. Snuggly cardigan and long dress
  B. Pinafore dress
  C. Flowy blouse and overalls

Favorite way to wear your hair?
  A. Braids
  B. Half-up half-down, long curls tied up
     with a ribbon
  C. Tied back in a bandana

Go-to shoes?
  A. Mary Janes
  B. Victorian-style ankle boots
  C. Wellington boots

Ideal purse?
  A. Illustrated canvas tote bag
  B. Fabric embroidery purse
  C. Wicker basket–style purse

Preferred colors?
  A. Neutrals and muted tones
  B. Ivory and soft pastel colors
  C. Earth tones

Mostly A: Cozy/grandmother style
You can never have too many cozy patterned sweaters. You love simplicity, and you are a thrifting expert! This is a very authentic Cottagecore style, and you've nailed it.

Mostly B: Woodland style
You could be compared to Disney royalty—imagine Sleeping Beauty roaming around her cottage home picking berries in the forest, or Prince Phillip wandering the forest in his dashing cape and hat. Someone in the woodland aesthetic would love long dresses and pinafores, favor the little extras on garments like frills and lace, and certainly lean into those romanticized European vibes.

Mostly C: Prairie style
You look like you live on a farm straight out of a storybook. This would include practical garments like overalls and Wellington boots, but also things like bandanas for your hair and aprons. You lean toward small floral or paisley prints in earthy tones. You remind others of characters from *Anne of Green Gables* or *Little House on the Prairie*.

Tie: A little bit of everything–style
Maybe you haven't defined your style, or maybe you like everything! Exploring fashion means you can try on as many hats as you'd like (and in Cottagecore, this can be quite literal)!

3

Engaging in the Cottagecore Lifestyle

*A*ppearances are a focal point of the aesthetic, but Cottagecore is a lifestyle, not just a visual style. This chapter will highlight how to engage in, feel like, and explore Cottagecore.

One of the key aspects of engaging with the Cottagecore lifestyle is the mindset you have in everyday activities. It's easy to zoom through life, not savoring the moments and just living on autopilot; this is why Cottagecore focuses on romanticization. Those practicing Cottagecore aim to take each moment and try to make it special, to enjoy the everyday pieces of life, and to intentionally feel their emotions and notice the things around them.

Use your imagination. If you're caught in the rain, instead of being upset, think about how you can make the moment magical. Everything that happens in the rain is more dramatic, romantic, and special. In each mundane moment that could so easily be brushed aside, refocus to see the mundane as beautiful. Watch the steam rising from your tea, see the patterns it makes, and enjoy the scent. Take in each moment as if you're the main character in the novel of your life. This doesn't mean there's only room for positive emotions; it means taking time to feel each emotion and seeing each season of your life as special.

Another fundamental aspect of engaging with Cottagecore is the connection to nature. Fully experiencing Cottagecore entails enjoying plants and flowers, wandering through forests and fields, and connecting with animals. Even if you're someone who can't keep a plant alive, that doesn't mean you don't have a relationship with the natural world. Here are some quick tips to help you connect with nature in a Cottagecore fashion:

Go on a nature walk as often as you can: If you're fortunate enough to live near a hiking trail, field, or nature reserve, make the effort to go explore! Look for wildflowers and try to learn what flora and fauna are common to your region. See what makes your area special! Even if you believe that you live in the most boring place, you'll be surprised by what makes your region unique. For example, in Ontario, Canada, we have a large population of black squirrels, and it wasn't until recently that I discovered they are an uncommon breed of squirrel! Now whenever

I see a black squirrel, I think of this fact, and it reminds me of how special nature is.

Fill your house with plants *(or start with one!)*: Try to learn their habits and what makes them thrive. Being able to pay attention to the details also leans into the slow living aspect of Cottagecore. You want to be able to pace yourself and focus on each moment, and looking after plants, things that operate at such a different pace from us, can help us take our own lives more slowly. If you're hesitant about plants, an easier place to start may be herbs! With herbs there is the added perk of the fruits of your labor—or the herbs of your labor, if you will.

Cottagecore Activities for Each Season

How would a Cottagecore enthusiast spend their day? A better question might be: What are the activities that bring you satisfaction and joy? Don't lose sight of any of your current hobbies or pursuits that bring you peace, happiness, and fulfillment. Those all contribute to your Cottagecore journey. But if you're looking for ideas for some Cottagecore activities to engage in, check out this list for inspiration in every season!

Spring

This is a season associated with fresh starts. The natural world is in bloom, and we are reminded that there are sunny days ahead. It is a time of renewal and rediscovery. Perhaps this makes it the perfect season to begin your Cottagecore journey!

LISTEN TO THE BIRDS

Enjoying each moment is a core element of Cottagecore, as is appreciating nature. Taking time to really hear the birds sing is a perfect combination of these two elements. Listen to their songs, daydream about whom they're singing to, and imagine where they're off to next.

MAKE A FORT ON A RAINY DAY

It can be normal to feel sad on rainy days, but April showers bring May flowers, and with this hopeful anticipation of beautiful blossoms, take time to indulge the day away and build a fort. This also brings back a childlike essence, evoking the feeling of a time when everything was new. See things through those eyes again, and use some blankets and pillows to create a safe space. Then watch a movie, or just listen to the rain against the windows, and enjoy.

DRAW/CAPTURE THE STAGES OF A FLOWER BLOOMING

In this season of growth, it can be so easy to miss all of the little changes that occur. Take time to appreciate all of the incredible things that nature does by capturing the stages of growth of a flower on a path you walk often. You can draw it at each new stage or take pictures. Checking back in on your flower will inspire you to appreciate the beauty nature creates.

GO ON A SCAVENGER HUNT WALK

Walk around your neighborhood, look for interesting new things that have come into the area this spring, and take pictures of them. A new blossom blooming, the grass finally looking greener, beautiful birds singing! Capture all of the spring freshness you can. Then take the pictures and make them into a collage, either physically or on your phone. Maybe it can be your new spring background, to remind you of all of the growth and wonder this season holds.

VISIT A FARM OR ANIMAL SANCTUARY

Visit a local farm or animal sanctuary in the spring—maybe you'll even be able to meet some baby animals! If possible, see if there is anything you can do to help the community or organization. These are often great places to get pictures as well.

Summer

When most people think of Cottagecore, the first place their mind travels to is summer: visions of running through a picturesque field, and golden washes of sunshine illuminating the space. Summer is the easiest season in which to engage with Cottagecore, and always the season when I feel the most Cottagecore spirit. But where to start? How do we practice Cottagecore in the summer? Here are some ideas.

PICNIC

Picnics are a quintessential aspect of Cottagecore. Grab a blanket and a wicker basket if you've got one, and invite your friends to enjoy a beautiful day. Maybe each friend can bring a different dish or snack! Spend your time finding shapes in the clouds, watch tiny ants climbing a nearby tree, take in the beautiful day, and celebrate friendship. Alternatively, make it an occasion to take some time for yourself! Bring a book or craft you're working on, allow your mind to be free of stress, and focus on the moment you're in.

GARDENING

Tending to a garden really captures the soul of Cottagecore. Spend your time outside with your fingers in the dirt, rooting yourself as a part of nature. Try growing veggies that you can harvest throughout the summer! Check in with your local garden center to find out what grows best in your climate. No backyard? Don't worry; you can easily create a balcony garden or even an indoor herb garden to satisfy your gardening itch.

FLOWER PICKING

Search your area for a flower farm! Many will have a pick-your-own option where you can create a unique bouquet! Are you going to make a color-coordinated bouquet? An artfully designed piece, or something wild and free? Bring a few friends and take some photos—it's a beautiful spot to capture memories! Maybe you can even dry the flowers you pick and use them to frame the memories you capture. No flower field nearby? There are a lot of invasive flowers that are considered weeds! Dandelions, buttercups, jumping iris. All can be very beautiful and allow you to appreciate the small things around you.

MAKE LEMONADE FROM SCRATCH

Did you know that there are many variants of lemonade across the world? There's the old-fashioned lemonade that we're used to in North America, but there's also Indian lemonade called shikanji, also known as shikanjvi, or Brazilian lemonade made with condensed milk! Take your time and try out a few different recipes from across the world, and see which you enjoy the most. It's a beloved drink, and universally recognized as the best summer refresher. Consider it your new warm-weather favorite!

PICK SOME BERRIES

Isn't the idea of finding wild strawberries and eating them off the stem just the most romantic thought? Finding wild berries can almost feel like time traveling! Just make sure they're safe to eat. If picking wild berries doesn't appeal to you, try going to a pick-your-own farm, and find fresh berries there!

Fall

That prickle of chill has begun to creep in, the brisk wind is changing the air, and the whole world is beginning to look, smell, and feel different. Autumn is here, and it's a chance to explore all your whimsies. It is perhaps the most beloved season, but how do we engage with Cottagecore in the autumn?

NATURE WALK

It's almost impossible to be sad in the autumn. Autumn may have brisk air and cool days, but is there a season that warms your heart more? Once it's in full sway, take the day to roam, admire how each tree's colors bloom slightly differently, and wait and watch for the leaves to slowly fall or wave in the wind. Indulge your inner child and sift through a leaf pile; maybe find the prettiest one and take it home.

HISTORIC HOUSES/LANDMARKS

Visiting historical places truly sparks the imagination, and autumn is the most imaginative season. Take time to truly see each place, learning about and imagining the people who made that place special and the memories that exist within those walls. Using your imagination and taking in new information are wonderful ways to engage with Cottagecore.

APPLE PICKING

Isn't apple picking just the sweetest of activities? It feels like one of those paramount markers of the fall. Luckily for us, it's definitely Cottagecore. Take your reusable bags and a healthy appetite to an apple orchard near you. Ride the wagon and enjoy the bumps along the road; something sweet is coming soon. Find the reddest apple first and take a big bite. The first is for you—the rest, apple pie perhaps? Also, most orchards have a farmers market nearby! A lot of locally grown crops will be for sale. Locally and ethically sourced produce not only elevates the Cottagecore lifestyle, but it also helps create tastier meals!

EXPLORE NEW TEAS

Coffee may be most people's go-to drink, but tea is the Cottagecore drink of choice. With so many varieties and flavors, there's a coziness that comes with tea that coffee or other warm drinks simply don't have. As the temperature begins to chill, go to your local supermarket or indulge in an artisanal tea store and try a few different teas outside of your typical comfort zone. Whether it be each morning or every other night, try to find a new favorite for the season. Look for teas from various flowers or plants, and try to taste the subtle differences in each one. There are also lots of adorable loose-leaf strainers and mugs one can enjoy tea with.

BRING A BOOK TO A CUTE CAFE

Cafes are really in their prime during the fall. The fall drinks, the atmosphere—the element of coziness is at an all-time high. Find a relaxing book and take it to your favorite local cafe—if you can see the colorful foliage, even better! With your seasonal drink, you can fall into your book and have the most magical day.

Winter

Winter can be the hardest season in which
to feel Cottagecore. The aesthetic is so often
associated with autumn, summer, and spring.
To illustrate the perfect Cottagecore winter, you
want to draw from those sweet and adventurous
childhood memories. Channel that energy into the
season, along with an extra dose of coziness.

SLEDDING AND OTHER SNOWY ACTIVITIES

Let out your inner child and enjoy winter by finding the perfect hill to sled on! It doesn't have to be for an entire morning, like what you did as a child, but taking a few runs down a hill will invigorate you! The rush of cold air and the bursts of laughter are impossible to ignore. Or if that's a little too adventurous for you, try making a snowman or snow angels. Feel the snow through your mittens; is it packy or powdery? Experience the childlike wonder of a classic snow day.

MAKE A READING NOOK

Winter is all about being cozy. And nothing is cozier than curling up with a good book—except for curling up with a good book in a reading nook. To create a reading nook, find a comfortable place to sit or lie down, then bring over as many extra pillows as you can. Create some ambient lighting, whether it be dimming the lights or lighting a candle, grab a snack and a drink, and then really settle in. Sometimes ambient music or a fireplace (real or not) can also help set the mood!

MAKE HOT COCOA FROM SCRATCH

We've all had the powdered stuff, but making hot chocolate from scratch truly is a magical experience. There are so many hot chocolate recipes from around the world ready to be tried! For something creamy and indulgent, try French hot chocolate and curl up with your favorite cozy film. Take some time to try to make the drink an aesthetic treat for the eyes too! Can you add cute marshmallows? Or an adorable mug? Or candy cane sprinkles? These little extra details will add to the experience.

JOIN A KNITTING CIRCLE

It can be hard to motivate oneself to go out and about in the winter, which is why joining a social knitting circle is such a wonderful idea. Spend time learning a craft that can help keep you warm during the winter, while also warming your heart with beautiful conversation and fun. You can find groups focused on other crafts if you don't like knitting.

COZY GAMES

Take out the classics, or try something new! Playing board games on a chilly day is such a pleasure. Enjoying the season while connecting with those in your home is a perfect Cottagecore activity. It's easy to fall back on classic board games, but there are so many new and exciting games that come out every year; there are even some board games with that extra Cottagecore feel to them! If you're not a board game person, maybe try something new like a cozy game on a gaming system, such as the Nintendo Switch.

BUILD AN ANIMAL WARMING BED

Engaging with nature is a crucial part of Cottagecore, so this winter, if you know that there are local strays in your area, try building a warming bed. Grab a large container or box and a smaller box that can be layered within the larger one. Fill the larger container with insulating material like straw, or warm blankets. Place the bed outside, especially on cold nights, so that local animals can have a shelter to keep them warm.

Crafts and Hobbies

Handmade things just mean more, don't they? There's a reason too! There is emotion attached to the craft, whether it's love baked into a cake or a perfectly imperfect knitted sweater. Taking time to learn a craft is a special way to engage with Cottagecore as a lifestyle. Throughout this section, we'll talk about some of the most Cottagecore hobbies and crafts that will engage you in the lifestyle.

One important thing to note is that starting a new hobby or craft can be challenging, and there is often some pressure to be great right off the bat. If we fail or are unhappy with our work, it can be so easy to give up, or never want to try in the first place. Just remind yourself that nothing has to be perfect, and you can always improve with time and effort. Remove the pressure of making something great and focus on enjoyment—that's Cottagecore.

Knitting/crocheting: Any yarn-related hobby is a wonderful Cottagecore activity. Start small and knit or crochet something simple. Maybe a scarf or tube socks. Engage with the hobby even further by joining a knitting or crocheting circle. Meet up with fellow enthusiasts who can encourage and teach you along the way.

Embroidery: Embroidery is a beautiful art that can be used to personalize any clothing or textile in your home. Have a pair of jeans? Make them Cottagecore by embroidering a mushroom on the back pocket. Or add some flowers to the collar of a blouse! This artistic expression introduces something unique to your attire or home, making things you already have a little more Cottagecore. Alternatively, you can frame your embroidery circles (or simply hang them up as is) as wall art.

Writing letters: This is one of the easiest ways to engage with Cottagecore. Grab your favorite pen—even better if it's fancy—and write a letter to a friend. Write about something going on in your life, or use your imagination—pretend you're a princess locked away in a tower, or you're writing to someone overseas. Romanticize the contents to add a little more fun! Once you're done writing, you can even decorate the letter or envelope with little stickers and illustrations.

Reading: Reading really is the ultimate hobby, isn't it? What else can transport you to a new situation, historical period, or world? Look for an atmospheric book, one that will make you feel cozy and Cottagecore. Any of Beatrix Potter's books will do; she's a classic children's author, and her books are Cottagecore to the core. Add to the effect by having warm drinks, tasty snacks, and cozy surroundings.

Scrapbooking: A huge part of Cottagecore is romanticizing your life and making every day seem special. Scrapbooking can help you look back at these times and appreciate the joy in them. Create beautiful collages and arrangements to help you see the value in each moment. There are also websites that allow you to create scrapbooks online! This is a little less Cottagecore but can be a good start.

Baking from scratch: "Made with love" is a saying for a reason. You really can tell when something has been made from scratch. Ask a relative or friend if they have any older cookbooks, or try to find one from a thrift store. Pick a recipe just by reading the description; don't look at any pictures—just use your imagination to determine what this recipe will taste like. Then start baking! Take your time and enjoy the process. By baking something without a photo reference, you can enjoy your creation without comparing it to anything else.

Painting: Painting can be an intimidating hobby to start. There is so much pressure to be good, and it's so tempting to compare ourselves to others. But you can do something just because you want to, just because it's fun. You don't need to hang your artwork up or put it on the fridge. Just enjoy yourself and take your time. Consider getting a painting book, so you can track your progress over the years. Paint what is in your heart, but if you need suggestions, consider drawing inspiration from nature; start with a flower or animal—something that brings you joy and comfort. To elevate the experience, try painting outside. Maybe bring your kit to the park and paint under a tree.

Which Cottagecore hobby should you try?

What is your ideal afternoon?
- **A.** Staying in and being cozy
- **B.** Walking outside, rain or shine
- **C.** Exploring and trying new things
- **D.** Testing out new recipes

What is your favorite accessory?
- **A.** A knitted headband
- **B.** Anything floral
- **C.** Something eye-catching—it changes all the time
- **D.** An apron

What would you want to receive as a gift?
- **A.** A weighted blanket
- **B.** Wellington boots
- **C.** A Polaroid camera
- **D.** Aesthetic cookware

How long are you willing to spend on a project?
- **A.** As long as it takes
- **B.** Maybe a day or two
- **C.** It really depends on the project
- **D.** A couple of hours here and there

Are you willing to spend time learning new techniques?
- **A.** Yes, I love learning complex things
- **B.** Not really
- **C.** Maybe over time, but I'd rather jump into something
- **D.** I can follow a recipe

Mostly A: Textile hobbies
Consider trying a textile-related hobby like knitting, crocheting, sewing, or embroidery! These crafts can have a bit of a learning curve, but there are so many ways to learn! There are books and videos that make the barrier to entry much lower. These crafts are perfect for cozy days. You can make gifts for all of your friends and family.

Mostly B: Nature activities
You love the great outdoors and being able to connect with nature! Check out a nature-related hobby like bird-watching, hiking, or stargazing. Maybe even create a nature journal to document your experiences with the great outdoors, to be able to keep a little bit of your passion with you at all times.

Mostly C: Social media
You like to explore new things and try a little bit of everything! Maybe you should document your Cottagecore journey on social media, so you can share your passions with the world as you learn and explore! Whether this be on TikTok, Instagram, or a blog, there are many ways you can get creative and share your experiences.

Mostly D: Baking or cooking
You're everyone's favorite person because you bring baked goods or a new dish with you wherever you go! Or maybe you'd like to be this person—and you can be! Test some Cottagecore baking or cooking recipes. Maybe try to make a nature-inspired cake, or learn to master making bread from scratch. Everyone will love how beautiful your home smells.

4

Cottagecore in Practice

*N*ow we have a firm grasp of what Cottagecore is, and how we can achieve this aesthetic in both our dress and the space around us. We have many ideas about how to engage with Cottagecore, so let's discuss how Cottagecore works in practice. What does Cottagecore really look like on a day-to-day basis?

Cottagecore in the City/Suburbs

Most of us will likely never live in a quaint cottage in the woods. Although it may sound like a dream come true, for many of us it's only a fantasy, whether this is because we work in a city or already have roots in a suburb away from the countryside. You may also simply know that a country lifestyle realistically wouldn't work for you. This doesn't mean a Cottagecore lifestyle is out of reach! It may surprise you, but not even this author lives in a small cottage in the woods. In fact, I live in one of Canada's largest cities, in a skyrise apartment quite far from any cottages. However, that doesn't keep me from identifying with a Cottagecore lifestyle. I've curated my space and life to incorporate the key Cottagecore elements. And I'm happy to let you in on how I created a Cottagecore life… without the cottage, nature, and copious amounts of puff-sleeved garments.

The best place to start is curating a Cottagecore space in your home. Yes, even an apartment can be decorated to feel Cottagecore! Take some of the tips from the Aesthetics chapter of this book and incorporate them into your home. Spend some time on Pinterest or Instagram and find some inspiration in how others curated their Cottagecore apartment. Make a vision board for the different spaces you'd like to focus on, and make lists of particular items you want to keep an eye out for. Without an intention of something particular to look for, it can be too easy to make impulse buys that won't really serve us or our Cottagecore pursuits. You have to be especially thoughtful about the space you have in an apartment, since it's more limited and you generally have less access to storage. For example, your office space may be tucked into a corner of the apartment, rather than encompassing a whole room. Consider this a challenge to spark inspiration—how do you make this small area feel like a Cottagecore study? It can be as simple as adding a small stack of books to your TV stand or hanging a gallery wall featuring some florals or other cozy art pieces. Or you can get very creative, finding a vintage wooden desk from a flea market or Facebook Marketplace and adorning it with candelabras, vintage books, an inkwell, and a series of fountain pens. Use your imagination to romanticize your environment as well; yes, it may be your day-to-day office space, but it could also be your letter-writing station!

The same thought can be applied to all of the other spaces in your apartment! Think about the spaces you might not usually consider, like your bathroom, a very modern room which may be a difficult space to transform. Start off with something simple: add some faux vines or dried flowers in and around your shower space and replace your soap holders with a refillable, aesthetic container. This will add that Cottagecore spice to your small space. Or, if you have the capabilities to do something more extravagant, consider retiling your bathroom floor with a vintage-style tile or painting the walls sage green! If you're a renter, there are renter-friendly versions of these projects, like using stick-and-peel tiles or removable wallpaper! If you have roommates or live with your parents and don't have total control over your space, you can still make changes to the spaces you do control, whether this be choosing Cottagecore-inspired bedsheets or having a tall candle by your bed, even if it's just for show! These small touches can make a world of difference to your space and how it feels.

What if you're not ready to commit to redecorating your whole apartment or home? Create a Cottagecore nook! Pick a small area of your home, a corner of your living room, or maybe your bedroom or an outside garden space. Add a little Cottagecore essence to this space, just to test how it makes you feel, before you invest time and money into the aesthetic. Start small: Does transforming a corner of your living room into a little reading nook make you happier? Does having floral linen bedsheets make you wake up in a better mood? Do the fairy figurines on your balcony or in your garden make you feel whimsical? Reflect on those emotions and see if you'd like to continue feeling them. There's no timeline—just do what feels right for you.

Gardening is a wonderful and relaxing hobby, and it doesn't have to be just for those with a plot of land. Consider starting a balcony garden if you can. Growing tomatoes or berries is a great way to bring that element of Cottagecore into your home. Using fresh vegetables in your meals or making fresh whipped cream with strawberries from your own garden? That sounds marvelous. Don't have a balcony? Look for a community garden nearby that you can join. This can also give you access to more

growing space to harvest a larger crop, and maybe you'll even be able to meet some other Cottagecore people. If neither of these are accessible to you, try a window herb garden! Grow things like sage, rosemary, or basil and use the fresh herbs in your cooking. You can even dry them out and create a little stash of herbs to use, or put them in aesthetic bottles to make a beautiful, personalized gift for friends or family! It can be difficult to connect with nature while living in an apartment, so growing what you can in your space is a wonderful way to engage with this aspect of Cottagecore.

For city dwellers living in a small space, it's worth reminding yourself to consider all of the unique and interesting places around you. It's impossible to stay cooped up all day, living in an apartment. A lot of cities have old and romantic spaces and features you just have to spend a little extra time looking for! Most cities or towns have existed for decades or even centuries before you lived there. Are there statues? Heritage houses? Take a look! Even if your city doesn't have antique aspects, it probably has an art museum or botanical garden, which can make for the perfect Cottagecore day trip! Looking at my Instagram, it wouldn't be obvious that I'm a city girl. I hardly ever showcase the high-rises or modern parts of town, because those aren't the parts of the city I enjoy or see myself in, but you'd be surprised how easy it is to feel like you're somewhere else. I often get questions from friends who can't believe how many of my photos are taken downtown. This is especially comforting if your own space cannot be transformed into your Cottagecore dream. Take time to explore the city around you, to find all of the Cottagecore spaces you can spend your time in (even New York City has Central Park!). On a weekend, plan yourself a Cottagecore date out and about! I've created two perfect Cottagecore itineraries for you:

Itinerary 1: Sunny day

The next chance you get, when the sun is shining and the weather is nice, follow this itinerary and have an absolute dream of a day.

Start the day by packing yourself a little picnic—even better if you have a wicker basket to carry it in. Before heading out, take some time for yourself with your favorite drink, whether this be a latte from your local cafe or a freshly brewed tea at home. Embrace the chance to be with your thoughts and enjoy whatever it is you're drinking.

Don't think about your phone (or don't even bring it!) or any to-do list—just experience the drink. Wear your favorite Cottagecore outfit; be bold and try the outfit you've been dying to wear, even if it seems too dressed up for the occasion (trust me, people are looking at you less than you think). Then it's off to enjoy the day! Get started by visiting a local historical site or an old part of town. Enjoy the architecture—maybe snap some pictures of any aspects that catch your eye. Perhaps a wall engraving you never noticed before? Or the independent bookshop's new display? Use your imagination—what kind of romantic event happened here? Who enjoyed this place before you? You'll be surprised by some of the spaces within your city. Once you've had your fill of history, it's time to enjoy that picnic. Find a nearby park and sit underneath a tree. Watch the animals skitter around you. What are the squirrels doing? Can you spot any birds? Take in how beautiful the leaves are on the trees as they blow in the wind. Look for some wildflowers, pet some nearby dogs, read a book under the tree, or just sit and enjoy. There isn't anything else you should be doing right now.

Once you've had your Cottagecore date, come home and slip on your favorite pajamas, even better if they're Victorian nightgown inspired—sometimes dressing the part really does help. Spend the evening curled up with your favorite hobby and reflect on the day (maybe even journal about it!). Appreciate the world we live in. Practicing a Cottagecore life isn't just about the aesthetics of rural life, it's about the way you live your life: taking things slow, being intentional. It doesn't matter where you live, what your home looks like, or what you wear, it's the things you fill your day with and how you choose to see the world.

Itinerary 2: Rainy or chilly day

It's easy to be Cottagecore on a beautiful day, because it's easier to see the world as a beautiful place. But there's beauty everywhere, rain or shine, so here's how to spend a dreary day the Cottagecore way.

This morning will be a cozy one. Wrap yourself in a warm blanket and find a comfy spot by a window. Put on a relaxing playlist, and with a cup of hot cocoa in hand, spend some time peacefully watching the precipitation fall outside. Giving yourself time to rest and enjoy the show nature has put on is something we rarely get to do. Once you have your fill, it's time to pull out your apron and put on your

coziest Cottagecore outfit, one that you don't mind getting a little dirty. You're heading to the kitchen! Pull out your favorite cookbook or start scrolling Pinterest to find a unique recipe you've never tried before. Be daring—choose something that's a bit of a challenge, something decadent! Take your time. With weather like this, there's nowhere else you need to be! Be sure to document your final results with a picture!

Now that you've finished your delicious delicacy, keep those cozy clothes on and throw on a raincoat and tall Wellingtons—it's time to enjoy the rain! Listen to the sound of the rain against the hood of your coat, smell the rain, and let those old feelings of rainy days from childhood fill you. Dance through the rain, jump into the biggest puddle you can find, and get thoroughly soaked in the joy of this moment. Once you get a little cold and your play is done, warm up with a bubble bath. If you have a bath bomb, now is the time to use it! Bring in a fun drink and a book you've been working on, and soak for a good while. Once you're done, find the coziest pair of pj's you own, light a candle, and move the reading to bed. It'll be one of those nights where you'll stay up just a little too late reading. But you'll still wake up feeling rested from the most soul-filling Cottagecore day.

So, to all of those who do not live in a perfectly quaint cottage in the woods, you can take comfort in knowing that a Cottagecore life is still very much within your grasp.

Online Community

It would be omitting a huge part of Cottagecore to not address the online community. Cottagecore took over social media, especially on Instagram and TikTok, throughout 2020 and 2021, and there is a huge online factor of the aesthetic.

My Personal Story

My personal experience as a Cottagecore creator is primarily with Instagram. Looking back through my posts, the first time I used the hashtag #Cottagecore was October 16, 2020. I don't think I could have guessed then where I would be now. I decided to try to connect with the Cottagecore community on November 2, 2020, by opening my account to become a public page and changing my Instagram to a business account. Having a business account allows you to see the analytics attached to your photos: the likes, comments, shares, saves, and reach (how many people saw your photo). This makes it easier to grow your account and opens you up to a larger number of people. At this point I had around 700 followers, mostly people I knew from my high school and university and other friends and family. I was already following many of the big names within the Cottagecore community, but I dove deeper into the hashtags and looked through the comments of accounts I enjoyed and found numerous smaller creators like me, people with several thousand followers or fewer, who were also hopping on the trend in the early days. I noticed that a lot of Cottagecore creators don't strictly follow Cottagecore style; they're often interested in multiple similar niches at once, like the academic niches—light/dark academia, vintage aesthetics, and princess-/royalcore. I personally put myself into the Cottagecore, academia, and vintage-style niches, and used related hashtags to grow my account. In growing in the community, I wanted to meet new people, at least virtually (we were in the midst of a pandemic, after all!), and started to spend a lot of time online getting to know some very wonderful people around the world who were interested in the same things I was, appreciated the same things I did, and were as excited about them as I was! Although Cottagecore is a rather large fashion niche, it is still a relatively small community, and seeing other Cottagecore-ers out and about is rare. Even when living in a city as large as I do it's uncommon, even in places that feel so perfectly Cottagecore. People in the real world tend to follow a modern mode of dress, and because of this, having that online community to share with and be inspired by is incredible.

I spent a lot of time throughout the lockdowns making little sets in my apartment and doing photo shoots with my sister. We always had so much fun seeing what we could do to transform a small space. Engaging with the Cottagecore community online also inspired me to go out and do more Cottagecore things: picnicking with friends at the park, trying to make frog cupcakes (those were a fail), or taking time to create elaborate "choose your own adventure" stories for my Instagram. These were all little things that I had wanted to do before, but I never prioritized them until I felt like I had a reason to. It felt so rewarding, because with each thing I shared with the world, I got positive feedback, encouraging me to keep pursuing my interests and creating things. This encouragement made everything more worthwhile, as it also made me feel like others were inspired by what I was doing. That is a really special feeling.

I'd still consider myself a micro creator, with just over seventeen thousand people in my community. Through this platform, I've been able to meet wonderful people, collaborate with brands I have always admired, and now write a book chronicling my perspectives on Cottagecore! The librarian in me, and certainly Katie from three years ago, is and would be pinching herself! My experience in the Cottagecore community has been absolutely magical. Every fellow creator or fan of Cottagecore is so kind and uplifting. I'm consistently inspired by those around me in the community. Cottagecore has impacted my life in such a positive way, and that is why it's so much more than a fashion aesthetic to me, and to all Cottagecore people. It's a lifestyle that brings joy, kindness, and beauty to those who practice it. If you're interested in keeping up with my Cottagecore journey, you can follow my Instagram, @chapters_of_katie. If you follow me after reading this book, please send me a message and let me know—it would mean the absolute world to me!

Starting Your Own Online Presence in the Cottagecore Space

Engaging with the aesthetic on social media can be relaxing and inspiring, but it can also be intimidating. There are many ways to immerse yourself in Cottagecore on social media, but here are some tips from the perspective of a Cottagecore creator.

The first thing you want to do is familiarize yourself with the community. Explore the

Instagram hashtags—you can use similar ones on TikTok as well. A few include #Cottagecore, #Cottagecoreaesthetic, #Cottagecorestyle, and #romantizemylife. There are many, many more, including those that get more nuanced, like #dark-Cottagecore or #Cottagecorewinter. There are many different niches within Cottagecore to discover.

Spend time going through different creators' accounts and peruse the comments to find other smaller Cottagecore creators; we all tend to follow one another when building a community. If you are interested in being known in the community and want to showcase your Cottagecore life, or would like to be involved in the community as an appreciator, engaging with accounts is a huge part of this. Responding to story content is a really effective way to start conversations or make yourself known. Try asking questions—creators are often keen to share advice to support your Cottagecore journey! It can also be easier to engage with accounts that have slightly smaller followings, as they're likely to be less inundated with messages, and you'll be able to build personal connections more easily.

After engagement, staying consistent with your posting is an important aspect of growing within the space. While being consistent may be challenging and time-consuming, it's crucial to developing a presence. Think of it like this: if you want to develop friendships or connections in real life, it can take time and effort! But with that time and consistency, you will see growth and friendships begin to form. This is how you can become a full member of the Cottagecore community on social media.

If you're interested in capturing your Cottagecore life and showcasing your journey on social media, but are unsure of what to post, here are some photo shoot ideas! You can try these to introduce your love of Cottagecore on social media. I also recommend putting your own spin on each of these suggestions—consider these your starting points.

FIELD SHOOT

This is the quintessential Cottagecore shoot, and an easy one to set up. Here's your checklist:

- *Big flowy skirt and a blouse, or a flowy dress (overalls can work too, if skirts aren't your thing)*
- *Lots of flowers, arranged in a bouquet*
- *Big sun hat*
- *Straw purse or basket*

Shot list:

Running photo - The idea of this shoot is to capture you running away from the camera in a field somewhere. Have one hand holding your hat and the other lifting your skirt as you run. You want to capture the carefree joy the space is providing you. The trick to this shot is the distance; you don't want to be too far from the lens, but if you're too close it may be cutting off too much of the field.

Sitting among the flowers - Take your bouquet and get comfy in a picturesque part of the field. Look for high grass or a nice old tree to sit against. Spread your skirt out around you, and you've got the perfect shot.

COTTAGECORE PICNIC SHOOT

This is the perfect shoot to do with friends! Grab a few other Cottagecore enthusiasts and create some beautiful shots. Here's your checklist:

- Big picnic blanket
- Picnic basket
- Aesthetic treats
- Decor pieces

Shot list:

Cheers - After arranging the picnic blanket, food, and aesthetic items, either by yourself or with your friends, face the camera with a glass and with big smiles. The trick with this shot is arranging yourself and your props to create an aesthetic tableau; you don't want a boring straight line. Play with the angles to get a unique framing.

Lounge shots - Stretch out and enjoy! Pull out a book or pose with some of the food you brought. The trick with this shot is looking like you're enjoying the calm and tranquility. Don't look at the camera—focus your gaze on whatever it is you're doing.

HOMEY SHOOT

Shooting in public can be scary! So not to worry—here is a Cottagecore shoot you can do right at home. Start off by finding the most Cottagecore portion of your space, and if nothing calls out to you, try bringing some objects over from around your space to create the perfect Cottagecore corner (remember, you only have to decorate what the camera sees!). Here's your checklist:

- *Cozy sweater*
- *Aesthetic mug*
- *Candles*
- *Cottagecore crafts*

Shot list:

Cozy - Sit down in a cozy, cross-legged position. Maybe hug one of your knees close to your chest while holding an aesthetic mug in your hand. Big smile!

Fixing your space - Pretend you're hanging a picture on the wall or adjusting a candle. You want this shot to look candid—just working on your perfect Cottagecore space.

Overall photo shoot tips:

- Seeing these perfect shots on social media can be intimidating. Taking pictures is its own skill, so don't feel like the things you create have to be masterpieces. Just try to highlight what Cottagecore is to you.

- Getting a phone tripod and remote are real lifesavers! Any of these shoots can be done without another person there to take photos of you with the help of a tripod. Tip for using phone tripods: taking off your phone case to set them up usually makes them work a bit better!

- Don't let crowds or strangers make you nervous when shooting in public. Ultimately, it's your life, and most people walking by you will never see you again and will not care or even notice that you're taking pictures. If you do feel nervous, though, see if a friend will join you. Having someone else around can help ease your nerves and make the shooting process much quicker! You'll feel comfortable whipping out your tripod in public in no time!

Cottagecore Places to Visit

Here are some Cottagecore places you might find in your own area:

Botanical gardens: Many towns have botanical gardens nearby; these are often perfect spots to engage with nature, and to see both local and foreign flora and fauna. Take your time and smell the roses, literally! Look at the individual colors within a flower and watch the branches wave as you pass by. Appreciate the effort and hard work that goes into curating such a beautiful space. On your way out, grab a social flyer; many gardens will have events that take place throughout the year, so see if there are any activities hosted by the gardens that might interest you.

Local historical sites: As mentioned before, historical sites certainly have that Cottagecore feel to them. Many people living in North America don't realize there is such rich and unique history in the spaces around them. Even if you live somewhere you consider boring, it may surprise you what history exists within your radius. Look up your town online, along with some keywords like "ruins," "historical houses," or "landmarks." If you live in a city, then what you might want to look for is local statues or art. You could be surprised by the age and history of many pieces in the area!

Farms: Farms are quintessential Cottagecore! Whether you go to a pick-your-own apple farm, a flower farm, or even a farmers market, there are always great Cottagecore vibes all around.

Parks/nature reserves: Visiting your local park or nature reserve is a wonderful way to connect with your local flora and fauna. Many parks also have signage explaining the local plants. Take time to actually read them and learn something new! Try to connect yourself to the landscape and your place within the ecosystem.

Cottagecore Places from Around the World to Visit

After exploring your hometown, you may be interested in expanding your horizons to visit some Cottagecore places from around the world! Here is a small collection of some of the most idyllic Cottagecore locations to add to your bucket list:

Giethoorn, Netherlands: Giethoorn is what one imagines a book of fairy tales must look like. Considered the Venice of Northern Europe, Giethoorn is a Dutch village about 1.5 hours away from Amsterdam. In this little town, there are no cars, only bicycles and boats. How dreamy! The village has beautiful, high-arched bridges, and each house is a perfect little cottage; it truly feels like you've traveled back in time when visiting.

Cotswolds, England: Widely considered one of the most idyllic places in Europe, the Cotswolds are a range of hills in southwestern and west-central England. This is where you will find the perfect collection of English cottages. The houses are situated among lovely rolling hills and medieval architecture. Many of the homes have a distinct yellow color that creates a cohesion in the villages. It's easy to imagine strolling through this truly beautiful place, wandering into small bookshops and getting lost among the rows of houses.

Charlottetown, Canada: Prince Edward Island, Canada's smallest province, is home to one of the most iconic Cottagecore literary figures: Anne of Green Gables. In Charlottetown, the buildings are quaint, with lots of mom-and-pop shops. It is a lush, green island, complemented by the unique red rock underneath it. A short road trip to Cavendish will take you to the Green Gables Heritage Place, where you can enter into the most idealized version of Prince Edward Island.

Cotswolds, England

Rothenburg, Germany: Rothenburg ob der Tauber is the Cottagecore maiden's dream come true. This picturesque town in Bavaria, Germany, truly feels like a step back in time. It's a beautifully preserved medieval village with the loveliest buildings and architecture. This town has unique treats called snowballs and is known for its beloved Christmas market.

New England Berkshires, Unites States: The Berkshires is a rural region in the mountains of the northeastern United States, with villages and towns scattered throughout. In the autumn it truly is a perfect getaway. You will fall in love with the rustic, small-town American charm of the Berkshires' quaint architecture and natural beauty.

Lauterbrunnen, Switzerland: Lauterbrunnen is a municipality in the Swiss Alps. It encompasses the village of Lauterbrunnen, set in a valley featuring rocky cliffs and the roaring, 300-meter-high Staubbach Falls. If you look at photos of this gorgeous location online, it's hard to believe it's a real place. A fairy-tale location for Cottagecore lovers.

Cottagecore Worksheet

REFLECTION
*Grab a notebook and answer
these prompts!*

What does Cottagecore mean to you?

What aspect(s) of your life brings you
peace and joy, or encourages a slower
pace in life?

What aspect(s) of Cottagecore do you want
to prioritize?

IMAGINATION
*Create three vision boards,
one for each category.*

Personal style: What do you want your
manner of dress to say about you? What
Cottagecore niche speaks to you?

Home: What can you add to your space to make it feel like your Cottagecore oasis?

Activities: What are you dying to try? How can you incorporate it into your life?

ACTION
Make it a goal to do five Cottagecore things per month. Be specific! Write them down in your notebook. Need some inspiration? Here are a few ideas:

Spend time in nature at least once a week.

Try one of the hobbies listed in this book; set the intention to finish at least one new project.

Plan a Cottagecore date with a friend.

Have a no-screen evening at least once a week.

Make a new animal friend.

Remember to be gentle and authentic to yourself and your values. Make an effort to live a slower and more sustainable lifestyle.

Farewell, kindred spirit.

We have come to the end, my friends. Thank you all for reading this book and showing interest in Cottagecore. It warms my heart to think of the Cottagecore community growing. I imagine each person in the Cottagecore community to be a unique wildflower, making the Earth a more beautiful, joyful, and wonderful place to be. Best wishes, and the fondest of farewells.

Katie Merriman is a librarian living in Toronto, Canada. Although residing in Canada's largest city, Katie spends most of her time romanticizing her life as a Cottagecore fashion and lifestyle creator under the Instagram handle @chapters_of_katie. Katie spends her free time crafting, sewing, creating content, and curling up with a good book with her two ragdoll cats, Olivia and Emilia.

ABOUT CIDER MILL PRESS
BOOK PUBLISHERS

Good ideas ripen with time. From seed to harvest,
Cider Mill Press brings fine reading, information, and
entertainment together between the covers of its creatively
crafted books. Our Cider Mill bears fruit twice a year,
publishing a new crop of titles each spring and fall.

"Where Good Books Are Ready for Press"
501 Nelson Place
Nashville, Tennessee 37214

cidermillpress.com